Looking Good

CLOTHING

by Arlene C. Rourke

Rourke Publications, Inc.
Vero Beach, Fl 32964

The author wishes to thank the following people for their help in the preparation of this book:

Dixie Montegomery, owner and director of a modeling school and agency.

Eileen Griffin, artist, illustrator and owner of a graphic arts company.

Library of Congress Cataloging in Publication Data

Rourke, Arlene, 1944-
    Clothing.

    Bibliography: p.
    Includes index.
    Summary: Advise for dressing the most attractive
way possible for one's body type.
    1. Clothing and dress—Juvenile works.   [1. Clothing
and dress]   I. Title.
TT507.R68   1986   646'.34   86-10091
ISBN 0-86625-277-0

CONTENTS

CLOTHES SENSE

Even if you don't say a word, your clothing speaks for you. Yes, it's true. Clothes communicate. What you wear and how you wear it can tell people a lot about you. Your way of dressing reflects your lifestyle, your hopes, and what you think of yourself.

Studies have shown that the way you dress affects the way others think of you. People who are well-dressed are generally thought of as being smarter, better-looking, and more fun than people who are sloppy in their appearance.

Clothing is no substitute for intelligence, personality, manners, and a good sense of humor. However, clothing does make a statement.

Looking good in clothes depends on how well you know yourself and how well you put together your wardrobe. You don't need a lot of money or a lot of clothes. What you do need is *clothes sense.*

Your Body

People come in different heights and sizes. Even on the same body, one side may be different from the other. For example, one arm may be longer than the other.

In order to be well dressed, all parts of your body should appear to be in balance. That means that no single feature should stand out and draw the eye to it. *The right clothing rebalances the body.*

Are you athletic and well proportioned? You can probably wear just about anything. There are probably no major flaws to correct. What are your best features? A tiny waist? Long, shapely legs? Great! Learn to play up those features. What are your worst features? Bulges? Too skinny? Legs too short? The right clothing can "fool" the eye.

Getting to Know Yourself

Find a room with good lighting and a full-length mirror. Take a good, long look at your body. Be honest. It's just you and the mirror.

The following drawings show the three main body types. You may not be able to match your body exactly, but you will get a general idea of what type you are.

Mesomorph

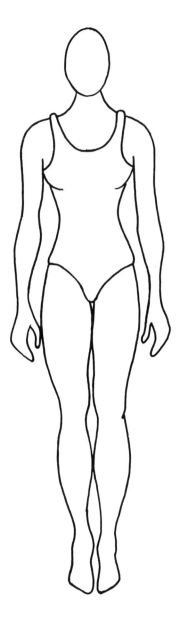

Mesomorphs have athletic, well-toned bodies.

Ectomorph

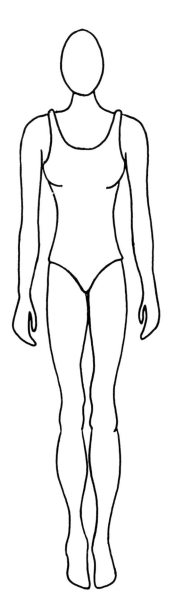

Ectomorphs are thin in muscle and bones. They appear delicate and fragile.

8

Endomorph

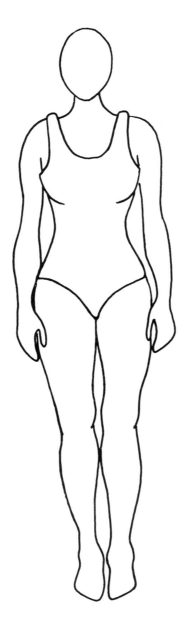

Endomorphs have round, soft bodies. They appear to have little muscle development.

Finding Your Style

To find your own style, you must first consider some important questions: Are you a sunny beach girl, a romantic, or a bookworm? Are you very feminine, or are you a tomboy? Are you a serious athlete, or do you shy away from sports? In what kinds of clothes are you most comfortable? There's no sense in buying a lot of dresses if you're the blue jeans and T-shirt type.

Remember, your style will be somewhat influenced by your body type. For example, if you are a romantic, you can probably wear lacy, Victorian clothes beautifully. However, if you are a romantic who is quite overweight, you should tone down the lace and ruffles.

TIP: Be yourself! Don't try to imitate someone else's style. It won't work, and you won't be happy.

Color, Texture, and Pattern

Clothes are made up of three aspects, *color*, *texture*, and *pattern*. When deciding whether or not to buy a garment, notice if all the aspects fit your style.

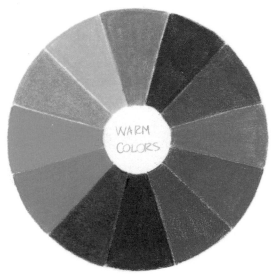

warm colors

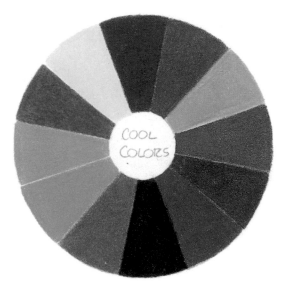

cool colors

Color: Reds, oranges, and yellows are called *warm colors*. They draw the eye to themselves. Greens and blues are called *cool colors*. They do not call attention to themselves. Dark colors make things look smaller. Light or bright colors make things look bigger.

Texture is the *weight* and *weave* (or *knit*) of the fabric. Texture can range from delicate silks to rough tweeds.

GEOMETRIC

POLKA DOTS

STRIPES

PLAIDS

NON-GEOMETRIC

PAISLEY

FLORAL

BATIK — ANIMAL

Pattern is the *design* of the fabric. The size and type of pattern you wear depends mostly on your body build.

14

Making the Most of a Good Thing

To make the most of a good feature, it is important to play it up with *eye catchers*.

Eye catchers

> warm colors
> big patterns and bold textures
> shiny fabrics
> glitter, sequins, or rhinestones
> fancy details, such as ruffles and lace
> jewelry and scarves

TIP: Never use any of the above on any feature that you want to hide.

If you're on a tight budget — and who isn't — set aside a few extra dollars for items that highlight your good features. Spend less on other clothing items.

For example, if you have beautiful hair, buy pretty hair ornaments. Use them to put your hair up in different styles. If you have a tiny waist, buy good leather belts. Novelty belts are fun once in a while. In the summer, macrame and rope belts are fun to wear with sport and boating clothes.

16

Making the Best of a Bad Thing

Now let's discover how you can disguise a less-than-perfect feature. The next several pages have suggestions for camouflaging, or hiding, defects. There are four general categories: *Too Thin*, *Too Heavy*, *Too Tall*, and *Too Short*.

Too Thin

Wear

warm colors and light colors — They make you
look larger.
medium to heavy textures
horizontal lines
gathered skirts — They give the impression of
fullness.
blousons — They make you appear more
filled-out.
blouses with breast pockets
bikinis — They are made for girls with flat
stomachs.
vests
wide belts
ruffles, pleats

Avoid

clingy fabrics — They only emphasize your thinness.
vertical lines
dark stockings — They make your legs look skinnier.

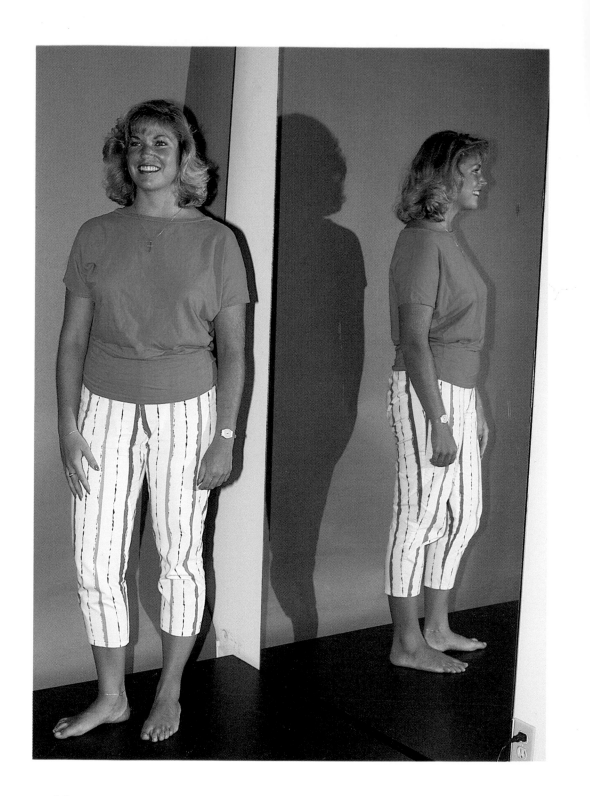

18

The second category is *Too Heavy*. With these suggestions and a good program of diet and exercise, being too heavy needn't be an insoluble problem.

Too Heavy

Wear

cool colors — They make you look thinner.

solid colors or small patterns — Large patterns would make you look broader.

smooth textured garments — Heavy texture adds too much bulk.

vertical or diagonal lines

tunics and overblouses — They hide a thick waist and broad hips.

straight or A-line skirts

one-piece bathing suits with a nice cover-up

underwire bra — You need the support.

belts the same color as your outfit

medium length hems

Avoid

horizontal lines — They make you look broader.

tight clothes — They make you look heavier.

baggy pants

miniskirts

low-cut necklines — especially if you have a large bust

bikinis — They call attention to your waist.

wide belts

bows, ruffles, or anything fussy and "cute"

The third category is *Too Tall*. This is a problem many shorter girls would love to have! Many professional models are quite tall. By wisely choosing your clothing and accessories, you can appear to be better proportioned than you are.

Too Tall

Wear
> heavier fabrics
> bold, large patterns
> two-color outfits — They cut the body in half at the
>   waist.
> flared skirts
> big tops, blousons, ponchos
> vests
> cuffs on pants and shorts — They make the legs
>   look shorter.
> cuffs on the sleeves of blouses and dresses —
>   They make the arms look shorter.
> wide belts in a contrasting (opposite) color
>   to the one you are wearing
> large jewelry

Avoid
> tiny prints — They throw your body out of
>   balance.
> ruffles and bows — They look too "cute" on
>   a tall person.
> vertical stripes — They only make you look
>   taller because the eye moves up and down.

The fourth category is *Too Short.* There are countless famous and attractive short people. Short is beautiful! Still, you may need some ideas to help you balance your proportions so you appear taller.

Too Short

Wear
> one-color outfits
> small prints and smooth textures
> simple straight lines
> soft, floaty fabrics
> stockings and shoes to match your outfit
> thin belts, the same color as your outfit
> simple jewelry, not too large
> ruffles, small bows, tiny pleats, lace

Avoid
> bold prints and heavy textures
> horizontal lines
> midiskirts
> cuffs on pants or shorts
> giant bags or other large accessories
> heavy shoes — They drag the eye downward.

TIP: If you're short, make an effort to keep your weight down. Extra pounds really show up on a small frame.

24

LET'S SHOP

Shopping can be a lot of fun. It can also be very expensive. You don't want to end up with a lot of costly "mistakes" hanging in your closet. When you go shopping think about what you now know about these things: body type, style, personality, good and bad features, color, texture, and pattern.

What to Look For:

quality — Does the garment look fresh and new, or is it already "shopworn"?

workmanship — Loose buttons and unraveling hems mean the garment is poorly made. It will not last long.

good design — Is it pleasing to look at? Does it suit you personally? Does the fabric suit the style of the garment?

What to Avoid:

anything you have to grow into or reduce to wear

anything uncomfortable

anything that isn't versatile — that is, anything that can't be worn with other clothes to give you different looks

light colored clothes or fragile fabrics which are difficult to clean

anything you don't feel good in

Ready to Buy

Let's assume that you've found a garment you like and you're ready to buy. Before you put down good money, ask yourself a few questions:

Do I really like it, or am I buying it because my girlfriend likes it?

Am I buying it only because it's "in" or popular?

Do the color and style suit me?

Can I get a lot of wear out of it?

Does it fit?

Do I look good in it?

Can I afford it?

If your answer to all those questions is *yes*, buy it!

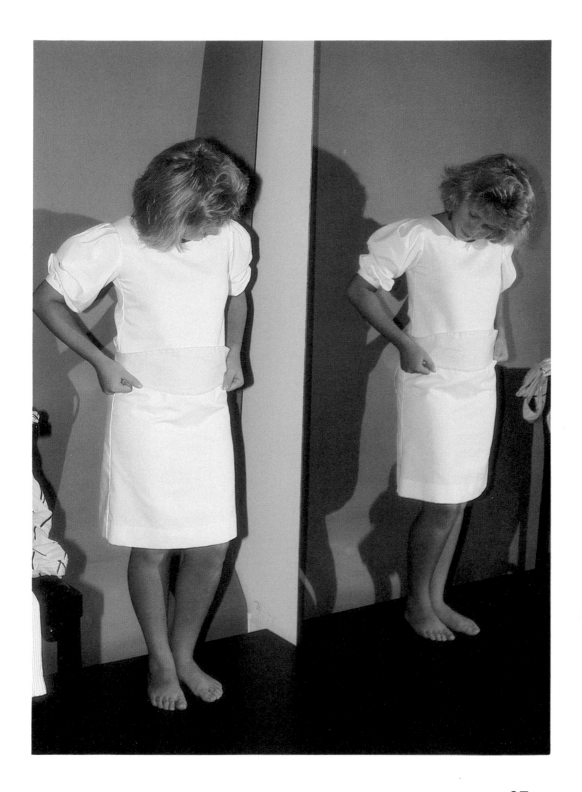

28

THE CARE AND FEEDING OF YOUR CLOSET

Have you looked inside your closet lately? Scary, isn't it? You probably have clothes in there that you've forgotten about.

Dressing well is a lot easier if you have a neat, orderly closet.

Here are some tips on keeping your closet at its best:

Make sure you have enough room. Go through *everything* in your closet. If it's too small, give it away. If it's damaged beyond repair, throw it away.

If the space is available in your home, ask your parents if you can store out-of-season clothes in a separate, unused closet. Or, pack them in pretty cardboard storage boxes with lids.

Make sure you can *see* everything. If you can't see it, you won't remember it.

Make sure you can *reach* everything.

Dividing clothes into categories makes things easier to find. Example: school clothes, sport clothes, dressy clothes.

Mend clothes immediately. Don't wait until you need to wear them.

Keep your shoes neat and polished.

Keep one drawer for socks and hose, one drawer for scarves, and so on.

BIBLIOGRAPHY

Real Clothes, J.C. Saures and Susan Osborn. William Morrow and Company, Inc. New York.

Dress Better for Less, Vicki Audette. Meadowbrook Press, Deephaven, Minnesota.

Dress for Health, Maggie Rollo Nussdorf and Stephen B. Nussdorf. Stackpole Books, Harrisburg, Pennsylvania.

The Complete Bonnie August Dress Thin System, Bonnie August. Rawson, Wade Publishers, Inc. New York.

Glamour's Success Book, Barbara Coffey. Simon and Schuster, New York.

Dressing Rich, Leah Feldon. G.P. Putnam's Sons, New York.

The Make-over: A Teen's Guide to Looking and Feeling Beautiful, Jane Parks-McKay. William Morrow and Company, Inc., New York.

Short Chic, Allison Kyle Leopold and Anne Marie Cloutier. Rawson, Wade Publishers, Inc. New York.

Fashion Smarts, Kirsten Brown and Susan Cooney Evans. Playboy Press Paperbacks, New York.

"Dressing for Class Photos," Seventeen. August 1985, p. 208.

"The Distinctive Looks of Denim," Seventeen. August 1986, p. 239.

Good Grooming for Girls, Rubie Saunders. Franklin Watts, New York.

INDEX